Amazing Escapes

Written by John Foster

Contents

Collins

Amazing escapes

Some people have amazing escapes.
They fall from the sky. They're attacked while
swimming. They get lost or trapped.

But they survive and are rescued.

Falling from the sky

A skydiver's parachute didn't open.
He fell 3,000 metres, but landed on a metal
roof, which bent as he hit it.

He wasn't badly hurt and was rescued by firefighters.

showing his broken helmet

Thrown out of a plane

A plane crashed into the Indian Ocean.
Everyone died, except one girl.

She couldn't swim, but clung to a piece of plane.
Rescuers found her after nine hours.

safe in hospital

Attacked by a crocodile

A swimmer was attacked by a crocodile in Africa.

His arms were inside the crocodile's jaws.
He bit its nose and it let go.

He was badly hurt, but
fishermen rescued him.

A crocodile's nose is soft.

In the jaws of a shark

A shark swallowed a diver's head in Australia, but he poked its eye and it spat him out.

He was hurt, but other divers rescued him.

The shark left holes in his wet suit.

Lost at sea

Three boys got lost in the Pacific Ocean
because their boat ran out of fuel.

They ate coconuts, drank rainwater and caught a sea bird to eat. They survived for 61 days until a fishing boat spotted them.

back home safely

Lost in the desert

A man got lost in the Australian desert while he was looking for gold.

He survived by eating ants and bugs, and was found alive after five days by local men.

the type of bugs he ate

Trapped in the snow

A skier was trapped in the snow after
an avalanche in the Swiss Alps.

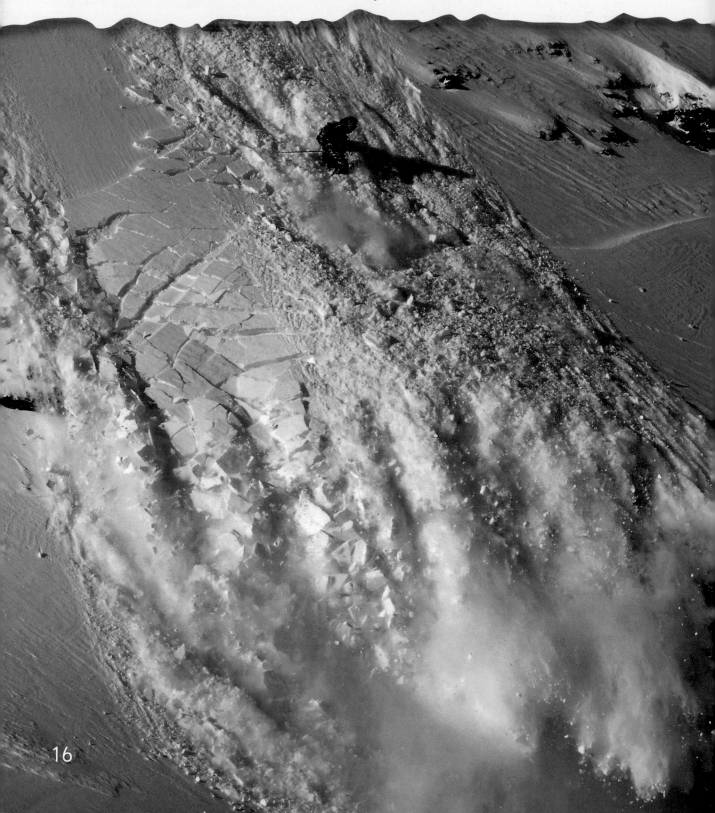

found at last

He survived because he was near the surface and could breathe. A search helicopter found him after 17 hours.

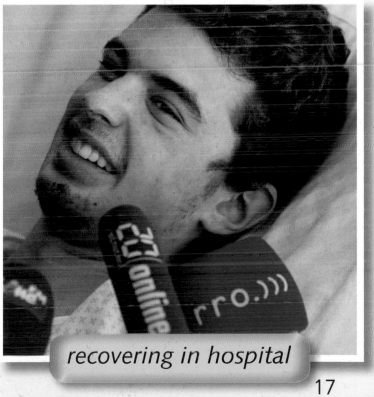

recovering in hospital

Trapped underground

Thirty-three miners were trapped in a mine in Chile for 69 days.

A tunnel was drilled and they were rescued in a small capsule.

a rescued miner

Lucky to be alive

These people were lucky. They were rescued and taken to hospital in time to save their lives. They all had amazing escapes.

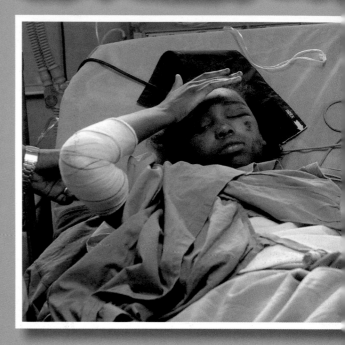

LIFE-SAVING LANDING

A lucky skydiver survived after falling 3,000 metres.

Swimmer bites back

A man escaped the jaws of a crocodile by biting its nose.

Three boys lost at sea

The boys were rescued after 61 days.

Lost in the desert

A man stayed alive in the desert for five days by eating bugs.

A REMARKABLE RESCUE

33 miners are rescued after 69 days trapped underground.

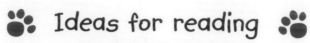

Ideas for reading

Written by Gillian Howell
Primary Literacy Consultant

Learning objectives: *(reading objectives correspond with Green band; all other objectives correspond with Sapphire band)* use phonics to read unknown or difficult words; reflect on how working in role helps to explore complex issues; use knowledge of words, roots, derivations and spelling patterns to read unknown words; use evidence from across a text to explain events or ideas; reflect independently and critically on own writing and edit and improve it

Curriculum links: Citizenship: People who help us

High frequency words: from, out, by, be, some, people, have, or, but, one, girl, nine, saw, her, him, his, three, boy(s), got, their, ran, had, with, them, after, man, five, an, because, could, were, these, time, last

Interest words: amazing, escapes, crocodile, shark, desert, underground, survive, rescued, skydiver, parachute, firefighters, coconuts, rainwater, capsule

Resources: paper, pens, pencils

Word count: 394

Getting started

- Read the title together and look at the front cover. Ask the children to describe what they see in the photograph. What do they think this man has escaped from, and why do they think this is?

- Ask the children to read the contents page aloud. Discuss the topics with them and ask them to say which one they think will be the most interesting or amazing.

Reading and responding

- Ask the children to read the text quietly. Listen in to the children and prompt as necessary. Remind them to use their knowledge of sounds and spelling to help them read words they are unsure of.

- Encourage them to look for words within words, e.g. the compound words *skydiver* and *firefighters* on pp4–5.

- Remind the children that information can also be found in the photographs and captions. On p5, ask them to say what extra information the caption gives.

- Ask the children to read to the end of the book. Praise them for reading fluently and support those who need extra help.